How Money is Made

BY MARI SCHUH

Rourke
Educational Media

rourkeeducationalmedia.com

MONEY & ME

Before & After Reading Activities

Teaching Focus:
Teacher-child conversations: Teacher-child conversations play an important role in shaping what children learn. Practice this and see how these conversations help scaffold your student's learning.

Before Reading:

Building Academic Vocabulary and Background Knowledge
Before reading a book, it is important to set the stage for your child or student by using pre-reading strategies. This will help them develop their vocabulary, increase their reading comprehension, and make connections across the curriculum.

1. *Read the title and look at the cover. Let's make predictions about what this book will be about.*
2. *Take a picture walk by talking about the pictures/photographs in the book. Implant the vocabulary as you take the picture walk. Be sure to talk about the text features such as headings, Table of Contents, glossary, bolded words, captions, charts/diagrams, or Index.*
3. Have students read the first page of text with you then have students read the remaining text.
4. *Strategy Talk – use to assist students while reading.*
   - *Get your mouth ready*
   - *Look at the picture*
   - *Think…does it make sense*
   - *Think…does it look right*
   - *Think…does it sound right*
   - *Chunk it – by looking for a part you know*
5. *Read it again.*

Content Area Vocabulary
Use glossary words in a sentence.

coin press
dies
engraved
equipment
inspect
U.S. Mint

After Reading:

Comprehension and Extension Activity
After reading the book, work on the following questions with your child or students in order to check their level of reading comprehension and content mastery.

1. *Describe the steps involved in producing money.* (Summarize)
2. *Where are coins made in the United States?* (Asking Questions)
3. *What are some things workers do to make coins and bills?* (Asking Questions)
4. *If you could design a new dollar bill, what would it look like?* (Text to Self Connection)

Extension Activity
Design Your Own Coins! Be creative by drawing your very own coin designs. Have an adult help you find a plastic drinking cup or a mug. Put the cup or mug upside down on a piece of paper. Using a pencil or pen, trace around the cup to make a large circle. Repeat a few times so you have a few large circles. Then gather a handful of pennies, nickels, dimes, and quarters. Look closely at the design on each type of coin. Look at the front and back of each coin. What would you change about these coins? What would you keep the same? Draw some of your design ideas inside the large circles. What do you like best about your new coin designs?

Table of Contents

Rourke
Educational Media
rourkeeducationalmedia.com

Making Money

Making money takes time. It takes lots of people and **equipment**.

5

Making Coins

American coins are made at the **U.S. Mint.**

Coin designs go on metal **dies**.

The dies are part of a **coin press**. It stamps the design onto blank coins.

The new coins are counted. They are put into bags. They are sent to banks.

A security guard protects the bags of money.

Making Bills

A bill design is **engraved** onto metal plates.

Ink is added to the plates.

The plates go in printing machines.
The machines print sheets of money.

Money is printed on big sheets of strong paper.

Workers **inspect** the sheets.

Bills printed with errors are destroyed.

The sheets are stacked into piles.

They are cut into bills.

Photo Glossary

 **coin press** (koin pres): A machine that stamps designs onto small blank discs to make coins.

 **dies** (dyes): Parts of coin presses that have designs on them.

 **engraved** (en-GRAYVED): When bill designs are engraved, they are cut onto metal plates.

 **equipment** (i-KWIP-muhnt): The machines and tools needed for a certain job.

 **inspect** (in-SPEKT): To look at something closely and carefully.

 **U.S. Mint** (yoo-SS mint): Six official places in the United States where coins are made.

Index

Further Reading

Fitzgerald, Lee, *Pennies!*, PowerKids Press, 2016.

Higgins, Nadia, *What Is Money?*, Jump!, 2017.

Jozefowicz, Chris, *10 Fascinating Facts About Dollar Bills*,
    Children's Press, 2017.

Meet The Author!
www.meetREMauthors.com

Show What You Know

1. What kinds of machines are used to make money?

2. What happens to coins after they are counted?

3. What are the first steps to making dollar bills?

About the Author

Mari Schuh is the author of more than 300 nonfiction books for beginning readers, including many books about food, animals, and money. She lives with her husband in her hometown of Fairmont, Minnesota. You can learn more at her website: www.marischuh.com.

www.rourkeeducationalmedia.com

PHOTO CREDITS: Cover and Title Page ©Kristoffer Tripplaar/Alamy Stock Photo, Cover and Pages 3, 4, 6, 8, 10, 12, 14, 16, 18, 20 ©Oksancia, Page 13 ©Jim West/Alamy Stock Photo, Page 17 ©Kristoffer Tripplaar/Alamy Stock Photo, Page 21 ©Bjorn Wylezich/Alamy Stock Photo, Page 11 & 22 ©Kristoffer Tripplaar/Alamy Stock Photo, Page 15 & 22 ©Kristoffer Tripplaar/Alamy Stock Photo, Page 19 & 23 ©Kristoffer Tripplaar/Alamy Stock Photo, Page 5 & 23 ©Jim West/Alamy Stock Photo, Page 7 & 23 ©smithcjb, Page 9 & 22 ©Kristoffer Tripplaar/Alamy Stock Photo

Edited by: Keli Sipperley
Cover and Interior design by: Kathy Walsh

Library of Congress PCN Data
How Money Is Made / Mari Schuh
(Money & Me)
ISBN 978-1-64156-400-7 (hard cover)(alk. paper)
ISBN 978-1-64156-526-4 (soft cover)
ISBN 978-1-64156-651-3 (e-Book)
Library of Congress Control Number: 2018930394
Printed in the United States of America, North Mankato, Minnesota